DANGER
IN THE DESERT

Timothy J. Bradley

Consultants

Timothy Rasinski, Ph.D.
Kent State University

Lori Oczkus
Literacy Consultant

William B. Rice
Natural Science Author
and Consultant

Based on writing from
TIME For Kids. *TIME For Kids* and the *TIME For Kids* logo are registered trademarks of TIME Inc. Used under license.

Publishing Credits

Dona Herweck Rice, *Editor-in-Chief*
Lee Aucoin, *Creative Director*
Jamey Acosta, *Senior Editor*
Lexa Hoang, *Designer*
Stephanie Reid, *Photo Editor*
Rane Anderson, *Contributing Author*
Rachelle Cracchiolo, *M.S.Ed., Publisher*

Image Credits: p.51 (right bottom) Cyril Ruoso/Minden Pictures/Corbis; pp.4, 12–13, 15 (bottom), 16–17, 20–21 Getty Images; pp.12–13 National Geographic/Getty Images; pp.25 (left), 49 (bottom) iStockphoto; p.42 (bottom right) AFP/Getty Images/Newscom; p.22 imagebroker/Jochen Tack/Newscom; p.40 Evolve/Photoshot/Newscom; pp.30, 35 REUTERS/Newscom; pp.8–9 NASA; p.15 (top) Don and Shea Sorensen, Blue Corn Studios, 2011; p.51 (right center) Toedrifter/Wikimedia; p.49 (top) Stan Shebs [CC-A-SA]; p.16–21 (illustrations) Timothy J. Bradley; All other images from Shutterstock.

Teacher Created Materials

5301 Oceanus Drive
Huntington Beach, CA 92649-1030
http://www.tcmpub.com
ISBN 978-1-4333-4897-6
© 2013 Teacher Created Materials, Inc.
Made in China
Nordica.112016.CA21601787

Table of Contents

vulture

The Dangerous Desert

The desert is a harsh place. The sun feels hotter under the dry wind. The land is **parched** and cracked, with little food for those who may try to survive there. A desert is an area that gets less than 10 inches of rain or snow per year. It is a hostile place for anyone—plant or animal. But the desert is not deserted. Thousands of **species** call it home.

THINK LINK

→ What are some ways plants and animals have adapted to survive in the desert?

→ How are desert plants and animals alike and different?

→ What are the biggest threats to plants and animals living in the desert?

A Desert Is Born

There are many reasons why deserts form. Some deserts develop naturally over time. Others form because of human activity. Natural deserts tend to develop at high **altitudes** where the air is thin and dry. Fewer plants grow in these conditions. Fewer plants means more sunlight hits the ground. The earth grows hot and dry, creating a desert.

Deforestation can also cause deserts to form. When large areas of trees are cut down, an empty field is left behind. Wind blows away soil. Plants cannot grow without soil. Without plants, only a desert can grow.

Some of the world's greatest deserts were once great forests.

Side by Side

Deserts often form near mountains. A tall mountain range blocks the cool, moist ocean breeze from the land on the other side. This creates very dry conditions.

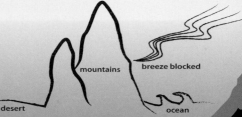

desert | mountains | breeze blocked | ocean

Desertification

Deserts can be dangerous places for those who live in them. But they also affect people who don't live anywhere near a desert. When **desertification** happens, the land supports less life. That puts us all at risk. Humans can't grow crops. And if we can't grow crops, we can't eat. Animals lose their water supply because land dries up. Species can die out. Scientists around the world are studying our deserts closely. They track how much of the world is in danger of desertification.

the Aral Sea in Uzbekistan, 2000

Scientists use satellites to view Earth from above. By taking measurements over time, they can see how the land is changing. These photographs show a lake shrinking. The land is drying out, causing the lake to get smaller and smaller.

Eleven Years Later

the Aral Sea in Uzbekistan, 2011

Nearly 25 percent of the land on Earth is experiencing desertification.

Desert Animals

Each type of desert animal faces its own challenges. Mammals in the desert must cope with high temperatures and little water. They often digest food quickly and need to eat often. Their **warm-blooded** bodies require lots of water to control their body temperature.

Reptiles, such as lizards and snakes, often make their homes in the desert. Because they are **cold-blooded**, they use the sun to warm up. Cooling scales cover their bodies. When desert conditions become too difficult, they become **dormant**. They can live off the water and nutrients stored in their bodies.

Insects and spiders live almost everywhere on Earth. They can be found among the hot sand and rocks in deserts. They have hard **exoskeletons** on their bodies, which help keep water inside.

The desert is home to animals that can't be found anywhere else on Earth.

It's All in the Hump

Camels are famous for their ability to survive in the desert. They can go without water for days and are useful for carrying heavy loads.

Giant Desert Hairy Scorpion

This large **arthropod** avoids the sun. The giant desert hairy scorpion likes to hide under rocks or underground to avoid the heat of the desert. It gets its name from the hairs that cover its body. These hairs sense vibrations in the dirt and help the scorpion find its **prey**. At six inches long, this scorpion is large enough to catch and eat lizards, snakes, and even other scorpions. The front claws crush prey. The large stinger at the end of the tail shoots **venom**. Scorpion venom **paralyzes** or kills.

The Desert Diet

Scorpions can live many months without water. They can survive up to a year without food.

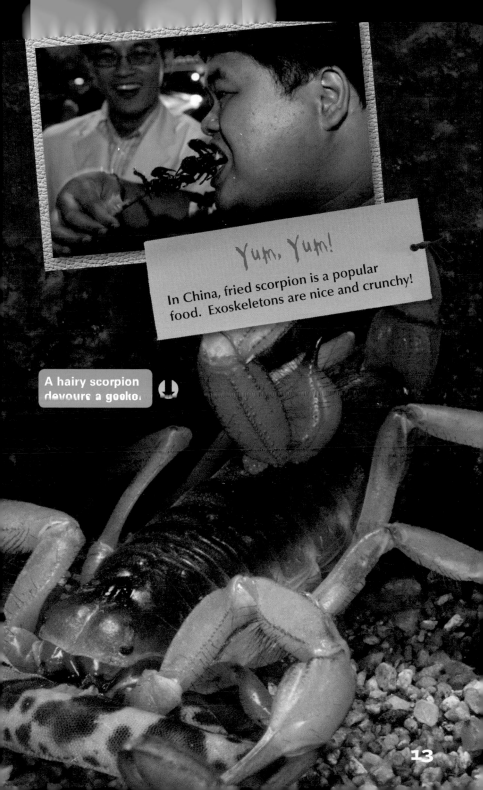

Yum, Yum!

In China, fried scorpion is a popular food. Exoskeletons are nice and crunchy!

A hairy scorpion devours a gecko.

Greater Roadrunner

The greater roadrunner can fly, but it prefers to run on the ground with its strong legs. This two-foot-long bird can be found in North American deserts racing across the rocky terrain in search of a meal. The roadrunner feeds on insects, reptiles, and small birds. Greater roadrunners can run about 20 miles per hour when chasing prey. They grab their prey in their strong beaks and beat it against the ground until it's dead.

A Famous Bird

Roadrunners appeared in many stories told by cowboys. There is even a famous cartoon character based on the roadrunner. Beep! Beep!

14

a young roadrunner eating a lizard →

Speed Demon

The roadrunner may be a fast runner, but the gold medal for speedy birds goes to the ostrich. This big bird can run over 40 miles per hour!

The roadrunner uses its long tail to help steer while it runs.

Sidewinder

In the same way someone might tiptoe barefoot over a hot sidewalk, the sidewinder moves carefully across the sand. It winds its way through the desert, touching the ground in only two places at a time. This odd motion leaves a curved path in the sand and keeps the snake cooler.

The sidewinder uses a rattle at the end of its tail to warn off potential attackers. Adults use their tails as a kind of **lure**. To a hungry desert animal, the tail can look like a tasty caterpillar or moth. The unsuspecting animal may move closer to find a meal. But one deadly bite from the sidewinder will prove the prey wrong.

direction of movement

point of contact with the sand

The sidewinder's bite can kill a human.

Snake Origins

There aren't a lot of snake fossils available because their remains are not easily preserved. But scientists believe they may have evolved from underground lizards.

DIG DEEPER!

Jawbreaker

Snakes can't chew their food. Instead, they must swallow it whole. A lower jaw made of two separate pieces, one on each side of the head, allows a snake to swallow food much larger than its head. Large pythons are able to kill and eat a deer…or a human.

The snake's saliva softens the prey.

Snake jaws expand to eat larger prey.

The snake's teeth move back and forth across the prey as it moves into the **gullet**.

The snake's skin and organs expand to accommodate the size of its prey.

Fangs inject venom into the prey, which begins the digestive process.

The gullet and stomach muscles are very strong and help move the prey farther into the body.

After the food is digested, the snake's organs shrink back to their original size.

The snake's body temperature rises, which speeds up digestion.

This illustration shows the process of a snake eating a deer.

Dingo

Dingoes are dogs that live in the harsh **outback** of Australia. They were brought there on ships from Asia thousands of years ago. Since then, they have lived apart from people and tame dogs. Living on their own, they became a new species of dog—a *wild* dog.

Dingoes are the largest **predators** in Australia. They are thought to be the reason many native Australian animals are now **extinct**. Lizards, insects, and mammals are their favorite prey. Dingoes are smart, fast learners. Sometimes, they work in groups. Together, they can bring down large, fast animals like kangaroos.

A family of wolf cubs can't find their mother.

Humans care for the wolf cubs. They're too cute to leave alone.

Wild Again

People have lived with dogs for thousands of years. No one knows for sure how it happened, but over time, dogs became **domesticated**. We use them to help make our lives more comfortable. Here's what may have happened.

Humans protect the wolves that are most helpful and friendly. These wolves have more cubs, which are welcomed by the humans.

Over time, wolves become more dog-like. They start living with humans all the time.

Other wolves visit humans. They enjoy eating the humans' leftovers.

When left alone, the dogs become wild again. Over thousands of years, fierce dingoes evolve.

21

These long-legged predatory birds stalk the desert and **scrubland** in Africa. They search for mammals, reptiles, and insects to eat. Secretary birds stand about four feet tall. They are gray, black, and white, with a bright red face.

These birds find prey by stomping on the ground. They startle small animals and insects into running. Then, they strike their prey with their hooked beaks and swallow it whole.

Flightless Birds

Secretary birds spend much of their time on the ground but still have the ability to fly. Some birds can't fly at all. Penguin wings, for example, have evolved into flippers to help them "fly" under water. Kiwi and ostriches have wings that have become too small to be useful. Instead, they spend all their time on the ground.

kiwi

Hunting for History

Scientists study secretary birds to learn about the behavior of extinct birds. Ancient birds may have hunted in the same way as secretary birds do today.

These birds got their name because the feathers on their head reminded scientists of the pens secretaries used to carry behind their ears.

Sounds of the Desert

The desert is full of strange sounds. All animals, including humans, need to know which sounds are safe and which ones mean trouble!

Rattlesnakes

Rattlesnakes make a very distinct sound. When threatened, a rattlesnake shakes its tail as a warning. The sound of a rattlesnake sounds like a baby's rattle.

Bees

If you hear a buzzing sound, it could be any number of harmless insects. However, if you hear a lot of things buzzing together, it may mean there's a beehive nearby. Make sure you avoid this area!

Bighorn Sheep

When bighorn sheep are fighting for territory, they butt heads. This sounds a lot like somebody slapping two pieces of wood together. The bighorn sheep may look similar to regular sheep, but their horns are dangerous!

Coyotes

They might look like dogs, but coyotes can be very dangerous. It's smart to avoid them, especially when they're in a pack. Coyotes sound a lot like dogs, except the sound is more of a "yip" than a "woof." Coyotes also have high-pitched howls.

STOP! THINK...

- What do these desert sounds have in common?

- How do animal sounds protect the animals that make them?

- What sound would you make to protect yourself in the desert?

Flash Floods

Rain in the desert can be deadly. Sudden storms can cause flash flooding. If you hear thunder, make sure you aren't near a stream, even if the stream is dry!

Tarantula

Like other arthropods, tarantulas don't have backbones. They have exoskeletons that attach to their muscles. These huge spiders are great hunters. Their leg span can reach a massive 12 inches. They feed on insects and animals as large as lizards and mice. They use their fangs to inject venom into their prey. Although they have many pairs of eyes, they don't see well. Instead, they rely on sensitive **setae**. These tiny hairs help them sense the world around them. Some tarantulas have structures that make silk. They are located on their feet to help them climb and hold on to smooth surfaces. Some tarantulas have a layer of barbed hairs. They can rub them off when threatened. If inhaled, the hairs can kill predators.

The tarantella is a fast-paced Italian folk dance. It was thought to cure the victim of a tarantula bite.

Slurp!

Tarantula venom includes a powerful chemical that liquefies victims. This makes it easy for tarantulas to suck up their prey through their mouths, which are shaped like straws.

Burrowing Owl

Burrowing owls are found in deserts and other open, dry areas. During the day, these owls hide in the abandoned burrows of prairie dogs and other animals. They hunt from dusk until dawn, sitting on a perch above the ground. Their sharp eyesight and hearing let them sense the movements of prey on the ground. Favorite prey includes insects and mammals like mice. They wait until the right moment. Then, they swoop down on them.

great horned owl

Owl Lore

Cultures around the world regard owls in different ways. Some see this flying creature as a bad **omen**. Others view the owl as a figure of wisdom. Whatever **superstitions** there may be, the truth is owls are predators that kill rodent pests.

Eye Caramba!

Owl eyes are huge compared to the size of their skulls. Rather than round, they are tubular in shape. Because of this odd eye shape, owls can't turn their eyes in their sockets. They must turn their whole head to look at anything that is not directly in front of them.

⬆ burrowing owl

Bobcat

It may look like a house cat. But this kitty has a deadly bite. The bobcat is twice the size of the cats humans keep as pets. Bobcats can weigh up to 30 pounds. They have **tufted** ears and a stubby tail. Bobcats hunt from sunset to midnight. Then, they go out for a second time at dawn. They will eat anything they can catch and kill animals much larger than they are. They can take down prey with a single jump.

Close to Extinction

The Iberian lynx, a relative of the bobcat, is close to extinction. If it dies out, it will be one of the first big cats to die out since the saber-toothed cats. The saber-tooth cat became extinct 10,000 years ago.

Iberian lynx

bobcat

Spotted Story

Bobcats are featured in Native American folklore. In one story, a bobcat traps a rabbit in a tree and is persuaded to build a fire. The embers scorch the bobcat's fur. The legend says that's how the bobcat got its coat of black spots.

Like many animals, bobcats have found ways to live in many environments including deserts, forests, and human suburbs.

DIG DEEPER!

After Dark

You won't see many animals running around the desert during the day. Desert animals know to stay out of the sun during the hottest hours of the day. Most desert wildlife are **nocturnal**. These animals have **adaptations** that make living in the dark easier for them.

desert cottontail rabbit

Some animals that are thought to be nocturnal are actually **crepuscular**. These animals are most active during twilight when temperatures are milder.

bibron gecko

Large eyes allow predators to spy prey in the dark of night.

jerboa

Some nocturnal animals have huge ears. Large ears help keep animals cooler by shedding extra body heat.

fennec fox

Large ears also help improve hearing for hunting and avoiding danger in the dark.

Desert Locust

These big eaters are a type of grasshopper. They live in Africa, the Middle East, and India. Wherever they are, desert locusts are hungry.

Locusts breed quickly. Young locusts join together in **swarms**. A swarm may fly hundreds of miles at night, carried by the wind. A large swarm can destroy crops, leaving nothing behind for humans to eat. Swarming locusts are **cannibalistic**. A swarm of billions of locusts means there is always a food source within easy reach—themselves!

A Tasty Treat

Sometimes, the hunter becomes the hunted. Locusts may eat human crops, but humans also eat locusts in several parts of the world.

Take to the Sky

The largest known locust swarm covered 400 square miles and was made up of close to 40 billion insects. Smaller swarms can cover several square miles.

Scientists are testing a wide variety of methods to kill locusts.

Wild Weather

Weather is a powerful force in the desert. Locusts and other animals often find food after rainstorms. When the winds change, every animal knows to take cover. Most desert storms happen in the summer months.

Even the hottest deserts sometimes get snow, too!

Powerful Forces

Desert winds can be extreme, reaching speeds of over 100 miles per hour. Large dust storms known as *haboobs* can take over the sky.

Heavy Rains

Monsoons are caused by seasonal wind shifts. These changes can cause strong winds to blow between the ocean and land, bringing heavy seasonal rainfall.

Fast Changes

Too much rain can cause dangerous flash floods. The dry, rocky ground usually does not absorb much water. A flash flood can occur within a few minutes or hours of intense rainfall. As little as six inches of rushing water can knock a man off his feet.

Mountain Lion

Mountain lions are **ambush predators**. They sit and wait until the time is right. Then, they surprise their victims. They use their strong legs to capture prey. Their crushing jaws deliver a deadly bite to the back of the neck. Mountain lions will eat any creature they can catch, from tiny insects to mule deer.

Mountain lions rarely attack humans. But as humans move into their territories, they may become more used to people. These big cats may start to see humans as another food source.

Defending Territory

Like many other animals, lions fiercely defend their territory. They mark their living areas with a powerful scent so other lions will know to stay away. Some lions live in the same territory for decades.

Mountain lions live in forests and swamps, as well as in deserts.

Prey Possibilities

For nearly a year, researchers in Grand Canyon National Park studied four mountain lions to learn more about what they eat. The graph below shows what they found.

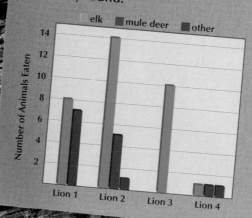

elk mule deer other

Number of Animals Eaten

14
12
10
8
6
4
2

Lion 1   Lion 2   Lion 3   Lion 4

Armadillo Lizard

This armored lizard lives in African deserts. When danger strikes, the armadillo lizard curls its tail into its mouth and rolls into a ball. Thick, square scales cover its neck and back. They keep it safe from the birds, snakes, and mammals that like to eat it.

Unlike other lizards, armadillo lizards don't lay eggs. They give birth to live young and care for them. Because armadillo lizards are small, **docile**, and easy to care for, they are sometimes captured and sold in pet stores.

armadillo lizard

Authentic Armadillos

Armadillo lizards aren't to be confused with armadillos. Armadillos are larger mammals found in North, Central, and South America. They have bands of armor called *scutes*. Scutes are made of bone that's similar to horns.

In Living Color

Lizards rely on their excellent sense of vision to spot predators and prey. Many lizard species use their brightly colored scales to communicate with other lizards.

agama lizard ➡

A Terrible Thirst

At home, you have access to as much water as you want to drink with a simple turn of a faucet. In the desert, nothing is more important than water. Desert animals have adapted to find water in places that appear completely dry. Some can go days without water. Some get their only water from the food they eat. And some never drink water at all.

The Australian thorny devil lizard has thin grooves on its scales. The grooves capture the dew during cold nights. The water drips into the lizard's mouth.

Some animals like the jerboa never need to drink. They survive on moisture from the plants and insects they eat.

Birds can fly long distances to find water.

Some desert animals live close to an oasis, or small body of water.

Most desert insects get enough moisture from their food to survive. Hard outer exoskeletons keep moisture trapped inside.

Plants in the Desert

There are certain things plants must have to survive. Land, air, water, and sunlight—take away just one of these essentials, and plants can't exist. The desert has plenty of land, air, and sunlight, but it has little water. Unlike animals, plants can't move to a shady spot. They must survive the heat of the sun and fiercely cold nights. They must store their water so it is not lost to the dry desert air. Some extraordinary plants have adapted to these very dry places.

Survival Secrets

The creosote bush opens its leaves at night to catch drops of moisture. During the day, it closes them to hold the moisture in. Long roots reach down into the ground, searching for water. Shorter roots close to the surface collect rainwater.

creosote bush

Most desert plants grow low to the ground. There isn't enough water for them to grow into large trees.

saguaros in the Sonoran desert →

cacti in bloom →

Barrel Cactus

Even a plant can get a nasty sunburn in the desert. The round shape of the barrel cactus helps it absorb water without getting too much sun. The barrel cactus often grows away from the sun to avoid a dangerous burn.

Many plants lose water through their leaves. To survive in the desert, cacti have sharp spines instead of leaves. The spines absorb moisture from the air and trap it. The shadows they make provide a small bit of cool shade under the deadly sun. Spines also protect cacti from hungry animals.

In Kenya, cacti are used for home-security fencing. The sharp spines keep out unwanted visitors.

A Prickly Problem

Spines, spikes, and thorns are found on many **organisms**. They discourage predators. A mouthful of sharp spines or thorns hurts. Predators may pass over a thorny plant in the hopes of finding a less prickly meal.

A large barrel cactus can store nearly 12 gallons of water.

Silverleaf Nightshade

The silverleaf nightshade is very tough—tough to kill. This plant is able to grow in soil with very few nutrients or water. It is poisonous, which keeps plant eaters away. The leaves and stems are covered with tiny, prickly hairs. It also grows **rhizomes**. These underground stems can make new plants. Even if the plant stem dies, the rhizome can grow new plants. A tiny piece of a rhizome can grow a whole new plant.

In dry areas, the silverleaf nightshade often grows spines and prickles. In humid areas, these sharp points aren't needed.

Noxious Weeds

The silverleaf nightshade is a **noxious** weed. It is dangerous to animals, crops, and humans. Noxious weeds can be found everywhere. Farmers and scientists work together to control the damage they cause.

African Welwitschia

A lot has happened in the last thousand years on Earth, and the African welwitschia (wel-WICH-ee-uh) has seen it all. This ancient plant uses its deep roots to survive in the Sahara desert. This adaptation is so effective that the plant can live for hundreds and even thousands of years!

In any language, this sloppy plant is a tongue twister. The welwitschia is known by African locals as *khurub* in Nama, *tweeblaarkanniedood* in Afrikaans, and *nyanka* in Damara.

African welwitschia →

Old-Timers

Some plants live just a season. Other plants have a much longer life span.

over 10,000 years
creosote bush

800 years
ironwood

300 years
baja elephant tree

200 years
ocotillo

100 years
boojum

50 years
golden agave

51

DIG DEEPER!

Protected Plants

These desert plants have adapted beautifully to the harsh days of the desert. Their lives depend on it!

Leaf hairs on sagebrush reflect the intense sunlight of the desert. These tiny hairs also protect the plant from drying out from harsh winds.

When water is available, the prickly pear cactus collects moisture in its spongy pads. Once the weather turns dry again, it can draw on the moisture.

Drilling Deep

Phreatophytes (free-AT-uh-fahytz) also grow long roots. The roots are called *taproots*. And just like the welwitschia roots, they grow deep into the land. Some grow as deep as 80 feet into the ground, looking for water.

The very small leaves of the rabbitbrush help it conserve water. Larger leaves would allow too much moisture to escape.

Desert Survival

Where are all these amazing desert creatures? One-third of the Earth is desert. The Sahara desert is the largest desert in the world. Located in Africa, most of this desert is simply rock and sand dunes. Plant life is scarce in the Sahara.

Africa is also home to the Kalahari desert. Much of the Kalahari is grasslands. It can rain so hard one day that it floods. But the next day, it is once again dry and parched.

Deserts Around the World

Check out some of the world's most famous deserts.

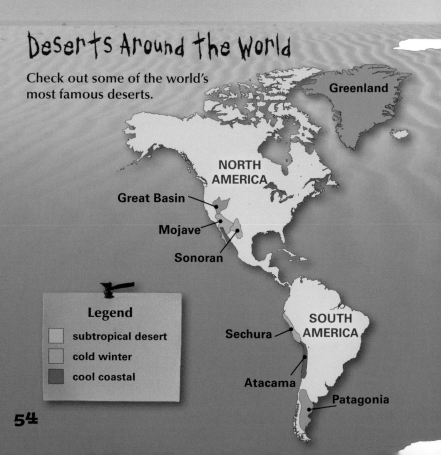

Greenland

NORTH AMERICA

Great Basin

Mojave

Sonoran

Legend
- subtropical desert
- cold winter
- cool coastal

SOUTH AMERICA

Sechura

Atacama

Patagonia

54

Desert travelers may wish for cooler temperatures. But not all deserts are hot. Some are dangerously cold. Antarctica is drier than any other continent on Earth. The dry air is unable to hold the heat of the day. Temperatures can drop well below freezing at night.

The Gobi desert is a large region in Asia. A bright blue sky, dramatic clouds, and snowy mountains lie beyond vast orange sands. Severe winds in the spring and fall make it difficult to travel across this desert— or survive.

ASIA
Qyzylqum
An Nafud   Garagum   Takla Makan
Syrian
Libyan   Gobi
Sahara   Thar
Nubian   Ad Dahna
Denakil   Rub Al-Khali
AFRICA
Great Sandy
Gibson   Simpson
Great Victoria
Namib   Kalahari   AUSTRALIA

Whether they are hot or cold, deserts are dangerous places to live. But the biggest danger in the desert may be people. Every desert creature has adapted to survive in incredible ways. Yet human activity continues to threaten the survival of desert plants and animals. New homes and roads bring a new kind of danger to the desert. Desert sand is fragile, and each species has adapted to live in precise conditions. When the desert changes, their chances for survival change, too.

People around the world are working to protect these unique places. Scientists are studying better ways to use existing land and water sources. Bushes and trees are being planted to restore desert sand. **Conservationists** are digging grooves in the ground to trap rain. Together, people are working to save the desert's secrets of survival.

"A desert can fool the eye. A sun-blasted plain of death turns suddenly into a landscape of sound, water, and life."

—Douglas H. Chadwick, writer

Glossary

adaptations—changes in the structures or functions of organisms that help them survive

altitudes—heights above the level of the sea

ambush predators—animals that hide and then attack other animals

arthropod—an invertebrate with jointed limbs and a skeleton on the outside of its body

cannibalistic—eats another of its own species

cold-blooded—a creature that's body temperature is controlled by the outside environment

conservationists—people who work to protect animals, plants, and natural resources

crepuscular—active during twilight

deforestation—the act or result of cutting down or burning all the trees in an area

desertification—the process of fertile land turning into a desert

docile—easily managed

domesticated—trained to live and work with people

dormant—not active, sleeping, or appearing to sleep

exoskeletons—skeletons on the outside of an organism instead of the inside

extinct—no longer existing

gullet—the tube that leads from the back of the mouth to the stomach

lure—a decoy for attracting animals for capture

monsoons—winds in the Indian Ocean and southern Asia that bring heavy rains in the summer

nocturnal—active at night

noxious—harmful or unpleasant

omen—an event believed to be a sign or warning of some future event

organisms—living things

outback—the hot, dry, remote area of Australia

parched—very dry, especially because of hot weather and no rain

predators—animals that live by killing and eating other animals

prey—animals that are consumed by others for energy

rhizomes—horizontal stems of plants, located underground

scrubland—an environment marked by shrubs and grasses

setae—bristle or hair-like structures on a living thing

species—a specific kind of animal; a category of living things made up of related individuals that are able to reproduce

superstitions—beliefs based on myth or legend

swarms—very large numbers of insects moving together

tufted—covered with hairs or feathers

venom—poison produced by some living things to kill or injure another animal, usually through biting or stinging

warm-blooded—having a body temperature that does not change when the temperature of the environment changes

Index

Bibliography

Eamer, Claire. *Spiked Scorpions and Walking Whales: Modern Animals, Ancient Animals, and Water.* **Annick Press, 2009.**

Did you know that today's desert scorpions are related to ancient sea scorpions that were as large as crocodiles? This book features six different groups of animals that trace their beginnings to the water.

Latham, Donna. *Amazing Biome Projects You Can Build Yourself.* **Nomad Press, 2009.**

Learn all about the Earth's biomes. Projects and activities such as building a cactus terrarium help you understand how important deserts and other biomes are to Earth's health.

Rice, William B. *Survival! Desert.* **Teacher Created Materials, 2012.**

You are lost in the desert and low on water. The temperature is rising, and no one else is around. What do you do? How do you survive? This book will tell you some of the most important secrets to surviving in the desert.

Ross, Kathy. *Crafts for Kids Who Are Wild About Deserts.* **Millbrook Press, 1998.**

Create a cactus puppet, a green toad paperweight, and other cool desert-related crafts. Just gather the easy-to-find materials and follow step-by-step illustrated instructions for 20 projects!

More to Explore

Conserving the Desert
http://www.defenders.org/desert/basic-facts

Learn about the threats to deserts from human activities and global climate changes, and how you can help preserve deserts.

Desert Animals and Wildlife
http://www.desertusa.com/animal.html

Discover fun facts about desert animals and how they survive in their extreme habitats. Learn about the desert food chain, and watch videos about fascinating creatures such as the tarantula and rattlesnake.

Deserts
http://environment.nationalgeographic.com/environment/habitats/desert-profile

Read up on deserts on the National Geographic site. Learn about life in the Sonoran desert and threats to the world's deserts. You can also view colorful photos of desert wildlife and take a habitat quiz.

Deserts
http://www.neok12.com/Deserts.htm

Play online games and puzzles as well as watch videos about the plants, wildlife, and mysteries of deserts around the world. You can also create a class presentation using images and information from thousands of photos and articles.

About the Author

Timothy Bradley grew up near Boston, Massachusetts, and spent every spare minute drawing spaceships, robots, and dinosaurs. That was so much fun that he started writing and illustrating books about natural history and science fiction. Tim also worked as a toy designer for Hasbro, Inc., and designed life-size dinosaurs for museum exhibits. Tim lives with his wife and son in sunny Southern California—one of the most beautiful deserts in the world.